OCTOBER,

OR

AUTUMNAL

TINTS

October, or Autumnal Tints

HENRY DAVID THOREAU

Introduction by Robert D. Richardson

Watercolors by Lincoln Perry

———

W. W. Norton & Company

NEW YORK • LONDON

Henry David Thoreau's "Autumnal Tints" reprinted from *Excursions*,
ed. Joseph J. Moldenhauer, Princeton University Press, 2007.

"Sunday Morning" from *The Collected Poems of Wallace Stevens* by Wallace Stevens,
copyright 1954 by Wallace Stevens and renewed 1982 by Holly Stevens. Used by permission
of Alfred A. Knopf, a division of Random House, Inc., and Faber and Faber Ltd.

For information about permission to reproduce selections from this book,
write to Permissions, W. W. Norton & Company, Inc.,
500 Fifth Avenue, New York, NY 10110

For information about special discounts for bulk purchases, please contact
W. W. Norton Special Sales at specialsales@wwnorton.com or 800-233-4830

Manufacturing by Toppan Printing Company
Book design by Mark Melnick
Production manager: Anna Oler

Library of Congress Cataloging-in-Publication Data

Thoreau, Henry David, 1817–1862.
[Autumnal tints]
October, or Autumnal tints / Henry David Thoreau ;
introduction by Robert D. Richardson ; watercolors by Lincoln Perry. — 1st ed.
p. cm.
Includes bibliographical references.
ISBN 978-0-393-08188-6 (hardcover)
1. Natural history—New England. 2. Autumn—New England.
3. Fall foliage—New England. I. Perry, Lincoln Frederick, 1949- II. Title.
QH104.5.N4T49 2012
508.74—dc23

2012012519

W. W. Norton & Company, Inc.
500 Fifth Avenue, New York, N.Y. 10110
www.wwnorton.com

W. W. Norton & Company Ltd.
Castle House, 75/76 Wells Street, London W1T 3QT

1 2 3 4 5 6 7 8 9 0

For Annie and Ann

Contents

Foreword

This volume has three parts. One part is Henry Thoreau's classic essay, or excursion, "Autumnal Tints," written as he lay dying. A second part is the suite of watercolors by the contemporary artist Lincoln Perry, watercolors on one of Thoreau's great themes, the glorious color of autumn seen through an insistence that "surely joy is the condition of life." The third part is a biographical and critical sketch of Thoreau's engagement with autumn and his coming to see it as a time, not of death and decay, but of ripeness, harvest, and new life springing from old.

What unites these three parts is their common aim to make you, the reader and observer, see; but each part stands alone in some ways. No one can beat Thoreau at what he does best, and no one need try. The biographical/critical essay sees Thoreau's essay as a hymn and a guide to victory, as a triumphant testament to how vision rises into the visionary. The watercolors are not attempts at botanically exact illustrations of Thoreau's text but something else. Botanical drawings may help one identify a leaf or a tree—and we have field guides for that—but even the best botanical drawings are Platonic types, typical leaves and trees, never a particular leaf or tree. Lincoln Perry's watercolors present and celebrate particular leaves, trees, and landscapes while he makes us see more than we usually do in the folds and colors and shadows of a particular leaf or the way one tree seems to give out light while another seems to draw down light into its darker self. We hope that the reader and observer can make from the three parts of this book a fourth, and his own, view—or perhaps even a vision—of fall color.

OCTOBER,

OR

AUTUMNAL

TINTS

ROBERT D. RICHARDSON

The Last Leaves of
Henry Thoreau

I. DEATH IS THE MOTHER OF BEAUTY

In February 1862, as the forty-four-year-old Henry Thoreau lay dying in his family home on Main Street in Concord, Massachusetts, in the cold New England winter, he roused himself to one last great literary effort. He knew he had not much longer to live, and the knowledge tightened his grip on the present. When his friend Harrison Blake asked him how the future seemed to him, Thoreau replied, "Just as uninteresting as ever." His friend Emerson maintained that "there is no release in all the worlds of God except performance." Thoreau also understood that no excuses would suffice for nonperformance. Certainly dying young could be no excuse. As recently as 1859 he had written in his journal:

I have many affairs to attend to, and feel hurried these days. . . . It is not by a compromise, it is not by a timid and feeble repentance, that a man will save his soul, and *live* at last. He has got to *conquer* a clear field, letting Repentance and Co. go. That's a well-meaning but weak firm that has assumed the debts of an old and worthless one. You are to fight in a field where no allowances will be made, no courteous bowing to one-handed knights. You are expected to do your duty, not in spite of everything but *one*, but in spite of *everything*.[1]

Emerson had also said, sternly perhaps but also comfortingly in "Self-Reliance," "Do your work and I shall know you."

With flinty resolve, Thoreau now turned away from the grand visionary projects he had been nursing of late, abandoning the huge Calendar of Concord that he meant to build up season by season, tree by tree, bird by bird, day by day, and detail by detail until it would flower into completion as an inexhaustible account of every natural happening in a statistically average year as lived out at the center of Thoreau's universe, Concord, Massachusetts. Thoreau now turned from this no longer realizable ambition to smaller projects he could still get both his hands around, stand-alone bits and pieces of the grand project. One of the chief of these was an account of the spectacular fall color in New England that he intended to call "October, or Autumnal Tints," and which belonged to a larger never-to-be-realized project he called "The Fall of the Leaf."

II. THE LAW OF DEATH IS THE LAW OF NEW LIFE

A common view of autumn, then and now, is that autumn is the time of dying and decay, the season of endings. We do not expect a "September Song" to be a merry one. Emerson's aunt Mary, a strict and brilliant Calvinist, accounted for fall color by insisting "it is the angel of consumption [tuberculosis] that dyes the cheek of fading Nature with such hectic bloom."[2]

But the paradoxical, counterintuitive idea that drives "Autumnal Tints," the idea that death is not annihilation and something to be feared but rather a necessary stage in the continuing cycle of nature, and thus something to be welcomed as much as any other aspect of nature, is quintessential Thoreau. The idea pops up on the first page of the journal he began in 1837, and by 1862 his conviction that "the passing away of one life is the making room for another" had been for twenty-five years a constant element of Thoreau's hot central core, the set of beliefs on which he habitually acted. This way of understanding death was first tested in Thoreau's own experience during the eighteen months from July 1840 to January 1842, which was easily the most emotionally tumultuous stretch of Thoreau's own life.

In July 1840, Henry's older brother John proposed marriage during a walk on the seashore with eighteen-year-old Ellen Sewall, the spirited, pretty girl from Scituate, Massachusetts, they were both in love with. That same month saw twenty-two-year-old Henry's first publications—a poem ("Sympathy") and a prose piece ("Aulus Persius Flaccus")—both in *The Dial*, the new transcendentalist magazine edited by Margaret Fuller. Ellen impulsively accepted twenty-four-year-old John, but she soon realized—she said—that it was Henry she really cared for, and that fact plus family pressure obliged her to quickly reverse herself and turn down John. Ellen's family sent her off to Watertown, New York, to get her away from the Thoreau boys. But then, in November, an undeterred Henry proposed to her by letter. This time Ellen consulted her father first and, at his prompting, turned down Henry. Ellen's father, Edmund Quincy Sewall, was an old-line conservative Unitarian clergyman who was actively opposed to the radicalism of Emerson and his friends, including, of course, both Thoreau boys. Emerson thought and said that the meaning of the life of Jesus is that all men and women have the potential for divinity within them; Thoreau already believed something very similar.

Radical changes of all kinds were in the air in Concord. Emerson was talking up a plan for a sort of free university in Concord. The Brook Farm experiment in communal living— a challenge to conventional views of marriage, of labor, and even of single-family homes was becoming a reality over in West Roxbury on what had been most recently a milk farm. Emerson was strongly tempted to join, but Thoreau noted in his journal in early March 1841, "As for these communities, I would rather keep bachelor's hall in hell than go to board in heaven." The Thoreaus took in boarders, and it was not a quiet household. On the contrary, everything in and around Thoreau's life was changing. His brother John's health deteriorated; it was the family curse, tuberculosis. On April 1, Henry and John closed the little academy they had been teaching in, and on April 26, Henry moved out of his family's house and in with the Emersons, who very much needed live-in help with their large house—known locally as Coolidge Castle but modestly rechristened "Bush" by the Emersons—and the growing Emerson family. Thoreau would live with the Emersons and be treated as one of the family for the next two years. It was almost exactly the amount of time he would spend at Walden Pond a few years later.

Living with the Emersons brought Thoreau closer to Emerson's second wife, Lidian, whom he adored and who was fifteen years older. He also wrote strange warm letters to Lucy Jackson Brown, who was Lidian's older sister and some twenty years older than Thoreau. When he had been nineteen and home briefly on vacation from college, he had thrown a bouquet of flowers through Lucy Brown's window together with a poem called "Sic Vita" that begins, "I am a parcel of vain strivings tied together . . ." Thoreau confided in Lucy Brown, he admired her, he fixed her oven door when it broke. He was plainly fond of her, but it was plainly as a son not a lover.

A few months after Thoreau came to live at Emerson's, a twenty-year-old young woman named Mary Russell also came and spent the entire summer living with the Emersons. Mary was from Plymouth, a friend of Lidian's, a frequent visitor to Concord, and, most recently, tutor and governess for young Waldo Emerson, who was four. There are admiring notes about her in Thoreau's letters and journals, and he wrote a poem for her called "To the Maiden in the East." Henry and his brother paid enough attention to Mary Russell to annoy other possible suitors, and if "To the Maiden in the East" is not a love poem, it is a pretty fair imitation of one. He calls on the maiden to "Believe I knew thy thought" and to "Believe the thrushes sung," and he says, with a sort of valedictory yearning, "Still will I strive to be / As if thou wert with me; / Whatever path I take, / It shall be for thy sake."

Between July 1840 and the summer of 1841, Thoreau showed strong feelings for and significant attachments to four different women, and that number does not include the strong-minded, passionate, and articulate Margaret Fuller (then just thirty-one—seven years older than Thoreau—and the editor of the brand new transcendentalist magazine *The Dial*), whom Thoreau took for a row on Walden Pond in May 1841, and who rhapsodized about the experience in her journal.

Concord in 1841 was full of young, energetic people who had yet to make their marks on the American imagination. They were all to become famous, so famous that it now requires a deliberate act of imagination to see them as they were then: untried, full of hope and new ideas, vigorous, eager for friendship, ready for love. They were young, Concord was young, America was young; no wonder the whole world seemed young.

Adding to the excitement of publication, the marked new interest in women, and the novelty of living with the Emersons was Thoreau's rapidly warming friendship with Emerson himself. When Thoreau came to live in his house, Emerson was almost fourteen years Thoreau's senior and like a much older brother to him. Thoreau had access now to Emerson's remarkable library, and he had Emerson himself to guide him to some of the books that would permanently shape his outlook.

So it happened that during this lively and interesting moment in Thoreau's life he came under the spell of *The Laws of Manu* via Emerson's copy of Sir William Jones's translation. "I cannot read a sentence in the book of the Hindoos without being elevated as upon the table land of the Gaughts [a plain near the Coromandel coast in India]." Coming thus suddenly upon *The Laws of Manu* (or *Menu*, as Jones transliterated it), Thoreau found it more impressive than the Bible. "So supremely religious a book imposes with authority on the latest age. . . . There is no grander conception of creation anywhere," he noted.[3]

Thoreau seems to have fallen into the book as soon as he arrived at Emerson's. By August 1841 he was so entranced by it that he had a moment of epiphanic awareness one evening. It was very much like Emerson's famous moment when, as he wrote, "crossing a bare common, without anything special in mind I suddenly felt glad to the brink of fear." Thoreau was also crossing an unexceptional bit of land that evening. Emerson's barn is perhaps seventy-five feet from the side entrance to the house; both are still standing, and the whole scene is still very much as it was on that August night in 1841. Thoreau's mind was completely focused on *The Laws of Manu*. Thoreau recorded his moment this way:

> As I walk across the yard from the barn to the house
> through the fog—with a lamp in my hand, I am
> reminded of the Merrimack nights—and seem to see

the sod between the tent ropes. The trees seen dimly through the mist suggest things which do not at all belong to the [Indic] past, but are peculiar to my New England life. It is as novel as green peas. The dew hangs everywhere upon the grass and I breathe the rich damp air in slices.

Next morning, as he thought about it, Thoreau felt the past assimilate into the present. Thoreau's young life and travels (Merrimack nights refers here to the events that became Thoreau's first book, *A Week on the Concord and Merrimack Rivers*) merged with the ageless lives of ancient India as recorded in *The Laws of Manu*. "The impression which those sublime sentences made on me last night has awakened me before any cock crowing. Their influence lingers around me like a fragrance or as the fog hangs over the earth late in the day.[4]

Thoreau's mature way of seeing the world, his conception of what it is to be human, and his strong personal idealism owe much to ancient Indic scripture and most to the *Laws of Manu*. "In the Hindoo scripture [referring here specifically to the *Laws of Manu*] the idea of man is quite illimitable and sublime," Thoreau wrote. "There is nowhere a loftier conception of his destiny, he is at length lost in Brahma himself."

What with the excitement of first publication, and his warm outgoing relations with sympathetic women, the companionship of the still-young Emerson, and now this blaze of revelation from ancient India—it was no wonder that Thoreau could write in September 1841 that he was living in "dangerous prosperity" at Emerson's. He was growing, discernably, every day, in emotional, intellectual, social, and spiritual ways. The days—Emerson called them "these flying days"—swept by; life was bright and eager, and new worlds of possibility swam into view like new planets. Thoreau was twenty-three, it was the summer of his life, he could see his way forward. "I want to go soon and live away by the pond where I shall hear only the wind whispering among the reeds," he wrote in his journal in late December 1841. "I don't want to feel as if my life were a sojourn any longer . . . it is time that I begin to live."[5]

A few days later, on January 1, 1842, Henry's older brother John cut a small flap of skin off his left-hand ring finger while stropping his razor. A week later the wound hadn't healed. Concord's Dr. Bartlett dressed it. On his way home, John had odd, painful sensations and was barely able to reach the house. Lockjaw—tetanus—set in on January 9. A Boston doctor came, looked at the wound, and said nothing could be done. John accepted his fate with Socratic calm. "The cup that my Father gives me, shall I not drink it?" John said good-bye to his friends and died in Henry's arms at two in the afternoon on January 11, 1842.

Henry sat in his parents' house silent and passive for days. Then abruptly on January 22, he too showed all the symptoms of lockjaw. (There was no cut; it was a sympathetic response but a terrifying one.) On January 24, Emerson's five-year-old son Waldo came down with scarlet fever. The little boy died three days later. Lidian, Waldo's mother, went into a long, sad decline; Emerson was desolate. When the young Louisa May Alcott came to the door to ask after Waldo, "his father came to me," she recalled later, "so worn with watching and changed by sorrow that I was startled and could only stammer out my message. "Child, he is dead," was the answer. "That was my first glimpse of a great grief," Alcott recalled. Another neighbor, Rockwood Hoar, "was never more impressed with a human expression of agony than by that of Emerson leading the way into the room where little Waldo lay dead."[6] Emerson was as ravaged by Waldo's death as Thoreau was by John's, but Emerson somehow knew he had to get it out, and he wrote letter after letter right after the boy's death. And in his journal he wrote, "The chrysalis which he brought in with care and tenderness and gave to his mother to keep is still alive, and he, most beautiful of the children of men, is not here. I comprehend nothing of this fact but its bitterness. Explanation have I none, consolation none . . ."

Thoreau, by contrast, was not able to express his grief directly and immediately, and the deaths worked upon him in half-hidden ways. Thoreau had been close to young Waldo, and these two sudden and early deaths rocked him and his world. As Emerson wrote in his journal, "Henry Thoreau had been one of the family for the last year, and charmed Waldo by the variety of toys, whistles, boats, popguns and all kinds of instruments which he could make and mend, and possessed his love and respect by the gentle firmness with which he always treated him."[7] Literally prostrated—shocked as he clearly was—Thoreau fought to find a way to accept what had happened. His efforts to express himself, not right away but after some weeks, and in letters more than in his journal, can sound forced, contorted, and unfeeling, but they are obviously meant to talk himself into accepting the deaths of John and Waldo. "Soon after John's death," he wrote Mrs. Brown on March 2, "I listened to a music box, and if, at any time, that even[t] [i.e., John's death] had seemed inconsistent with the beauty and harmony of the universe, it was then gently constrained into the placid course of nature by those steady notes, in mild and unoffended tone echoing far and wide under the heavens. But I find these things more strange than sad to me. What right have I to grieve, who have not ceased to wonder?"[8]

The deaths of John and Waldo also drove Thoreau to a labored defense of his youthful, untested, Emersonian idealism. He wrote to Lucy Brown in the same March 2 letter: "I do not wish to see John ever again—I mean him who is dead—but that other whom only he would have wished to see, or to be, of whom he was the imperfect representative. For we are not what we are, nor do we treat or esteem each other for such, but for what we are capable of being." It was the young Longfellow who once said that while others judge us by what we have already done, we judge ourselves by what we feel *capable* of doing.[9]

Emerson, idealism, and Thoreau's own proclivities led Thoreau to try to understand death in the context of nature. Once more to Lucy Brown, whom he must have trusted completely at this point in his life, he wrote, "As for Waldo, he died as the mist rises from the brook, which the sun will soon dart his rays through. Do not the flowers die every autumn?" This is not unfeeling or cold. It is a desperate, cross-grained, and extravagant effort to accept the unacceptable. A few days later in his journal Thoreau wrote, "I live in the perpetual verdure of the globe—I die in the annual decay of nature." Then he tried it another way. "We can understand the phenomenon of death in the animal better if we first consider it in the order next below us—the vegetable.[10]

Thus armed or prepared, Thoreau turned on March 11, 1842, to the unavoidable task of writing a letter of condolence to Emerson, who was dealing with his loss by throwing himself into his lecture schedule in New York. (While there, the still shaken and bereft Emerson went one day to the home of Henry James Sr. to admire the latter's newborn first son, William. What strength that visit must have required!) Quoting this letter in snippets makes Thoreau sound uncaring. A fuller reading of his letter to Emerson shows his real intentions.

> The sun has just burst through the fog, and I hear blue-birds, song-sparrows, larks and robins down in the meadow. The other day I walked in the woods, but

found myself rather denaturalized by late habits. Yet it is the same nature that Burns and Wordsworth loved, the same life that Shakespeare and Milton lived. The wind still roars in the wood, as if nothing had happened out of the course of nature. The sound of the waterfall is not interrupted more than if a feather had fallen.

Nature is not ruffled by the rudest blast. The hurricane only snaps a few twigs in some nook of the forest. The snow attains its average depth each winter, and the chic-adee lisps the same notes. The old laws prevail in spite of pestilence and famine. No genius or virtue so rare and revolutionary appears in town or village, that the pine ceases to exude resin in the wood, or beast or bird lays aside its habits.

How plain that death is only the phenomenon of the individual or class. Nature does not recognize it, she finds her own again under new forms without loss. Yet death is beautiful when seen to be a law, and not an accident—it is as common as life. Men die in Tartary, in Ethiopia—in England—in Wisconsin. And after all what portion of this so serene and living nature can be said to be alive? Do this year's grasses and foliage outnumber all the past?

Every blade in the field—every leaf in the forest—lays down its life in its season as beautifully as it was taken up. It is the pastime of a full quarter of the year. Dead

trees—sere leaves—dried grass and herbs—are not these a good part of our life? And what is that pride of our autumnal scenery but the hectic flush—the sallow and cadaverous countenance of vegetation—its painted throes—with the November air for canvas?

When we look over the fields are we not saddened because the particular flowers or grasses will wither— for the law of their death is the law of new life. Will not the land be in good heart *because* the crops die down from year to year? The herbage cheerfully consents to bloom, and wither, and give place to new.

So it is with the human plant. We are partial and selfish when we lament the death of the individual, unless our plaint be a paean to the departed soul, and a sigh as the wind sighs over the fields, which no shrub interrupts in its private grief.

One might as well go into mourning for every sere leaf—but the more innocent and wiser soul will snuff a fragrance in the gales of autumn, and congratulate Nature upon her health.[11]

Thoreau's letter is not a condolence letter, at least not a conventional one, and it is hard to believe that Emerson got much comfort from such a letter, with its contrariness, its self-involvement, and its poeticizing the tragedy. But Emerson would have known the offsetting facts of the situation. Thoreau had been literally flattened by his brother's death (unable even to get out of bed for weeks) and again by little Waldo's. Thoreau had also been unable to express his shock and grief. His letter to Emerson, when it came at last, shows a young man who can't or won't handle grief but is already taking the classical, stoic line that it is not to society, to family, or to God that we must turn for help, but to nature. Thoreau may have been poeticizing a tragedy, but he was already a person for whom poetry was a sacred road to wisdom, and he was prepared to live and to die himself by his growing conviction that death was the path to new life. This last was not, for Thoreau, a Christian idea, but the sort of idea Christianity had arisen to express. So it is not likely that Emerson will have misunderstood what Thoreau was trying to say. Emerson was now thirty-nine and had suffered greater losses than most. When he was four, his eight-year-old brother John died; when he was eight, his father died; when he was eleven, his three-year-old sister Mary Caroline died. Then, when Emerson was twenty-eight, his first wife Ellen, barely twenty, died; when Emerson was thirty-one, his twenty-nine-year-old brother Edward died; when Emerson was thirty-three, his brother Charles died at twenty-seven. And now there was young Waldo's death. Emerson wrote to Margaret Fuller: "My little boy must die also. All his wonderful beauty could not save him. He gave up his innocent breath last night and my world this morning is poor enough. He had *Scarlatina* on Monday night. Shall I ever dare to love any thing again. Farewell and Farewell,

O my boy!"[12] Emerson was profoundly acquainted with death, grief, and loss but somehow pushed himself through grief, not to despair but to take a fresh hold on life. Thoreau too was working himself into fighting trim. "Tis true as you say," he wrote to Isaiah Williams, "Man's ends are shaped for him, but who ever dared confess the extent of his free agency? Though I am weak I am strong too. If God shapes my ends—he shapes me also—and his means are always equal to his ends. His work does not lack this completeness, that the creature consents." Sounding now like defiant Ahab on the deck of the *Pequod* in a storm, Thoreau tells Williams, "I am my destiny. . . . My destiny is now arrived, is now arriving. I believe that what I call my circumstances will be a very true history of myself."[13]

Thoreau never says it in so many words, but his letters, to Mrs. Brown, to Emerson, and now to Isaiah Williams, tell the story plainly enough. In some way, Thoreau seems to have felt a kind of survivor's guilt, a sense that his new life has been enabled, perhaps even bought, by John's death, and he now felt he had to live and achieve and experience life for John as well as for himself. At the end of Simone de Beauvoir's first volume of memoirs, *The Memoirs of a Dutiful Daughter*, Simone's life is emboldened or enabled by the death of her best friend, Zaza, who, unlike Simone, had simply not been able to break away from her deeply conventional upbringing. Similarly, John's and Waldo's deaths have made possible this Promethean new Thoreau and his "I am my destiny." The moment is not just a personal reassertion of control over life but a vocational epiphany for the twenty-four-year-old Thoreau, who had just two more decades to live. The "true history of myself" he commits himself to here will come to fruition as *Walden* more than a dozen years hence, and it will also lead directly to the great essay "Autumnal Tints," which will take Thoreau back to the contemplation of death again, as his own drew near.

The deaths of John and Waldo, and Thoreau's astonishing, dismaying, and vigorous response to them set Thoreau's future course and ushered him into his real life. In his journal for March 14, 1842, the same day he wrote Williams and crowed like Chanticleer, he put the same thought in a calmer and more ironic register: "What am I good for now—who am still reaching after high things but to hear and tell the news—to bring wood and water—and count how many eggs the hens lay? In the meantime, I expect my life will begin."[14]

III. THE LAST LECTURE

Sixteen years later, Thoreau wrote his lecture/essay on death, the piece we know as "Autumnal Tints." The subject had never really left him. Almost as soon as he recommenced keeping a regular journal for its own sake and quite apart from other writing projects—that was November 1850—Thoreau began to catalog the fall colors. But now in the winter of 1858–59, he pulled a decade's worth of journal entries together, organizing them into a seasonal chronology and giving them as the lecture "Autumnal Tints" in Worcester on February 22, 1859. Not quite two years later, on December 11, 1860, at Waterbury, Connecticut, Thoreau gave the last lecture of his career. It was, fittingly enough, "Autumnal Tints."[15] In May 1861, Thoreau took his last trip out of state, to Minnesota. In September he made his last visit to Walden Pond. On November 3 he wrote his last journal entry:

> After a violent easterly storm in the night, which clears up at noon (November 3, 1861), I notice that the surface of the railroad causeway, composed of gravel, is singularly marked, as if stratified like some slate rocks, on their edges, so that I can tell within a small fraction of a degree from what quarter the rain came. . . . Thus each wind is self-registering.

So is each writer's mind, and in the early weeks of 1862 the dying Thoreau worked to turn his "Autumnal Tints" lecture into a printable essay. He sent the finished piece to Ticknor and Fields on February 20, 1862. It was accepted and set in type at what seems to us now as breakneck speed, for on March 11 Thoreau returned corrected proofs to the printer. On May 6, at nine in the morning, Henry Thoreau died. "Autumnal Tints" was published—came to life—six months later, in the *Atlantic Monthly* for November 1862. Once again, the law of death proved to be the law of new life. Had he not known that he was dying, and had he not accepted the fact, he would not have aban-

doned his grand Calendar of Concord project to settle for a few salvageable bits. Without the sure knowledge he was dying, Thoreau would not have pulled "Autumnal Tints" together.

IV. IT IS NOT ENOUGH TO SEE: YOU MUST LOOK

The finished essay is essentially a poet-naturalist's reframing of the old theological problem of the Fall. Thoreau has come to an intellectual position close to what Wallace Stevens will work out seventy years later in "Sunday Morning." "What is divinity if it can come / Only in silent shadows and in dreams?" asks Stevens. Divinity for Stevens is everywhere, but so is death, and death for Stevens is not cessation, but agent. "Death is the mother of beauty; hence from her / Alone shall come fulfillment to our dreams / And our desires. Although she strews the leaves / Of sure obliteration on our paths . . ."

"Death is the mother of beauty" could easily serve as the motto—or even the title—of Thoreau's "Autumnal Tints." The essay is concerned with the perception of beauty—the important word here is *perception*—and with how to teach ourselves to see more than we usually do. Thoreau's comments are practical, helpful, and profoundly cheering. His enthusiasm, his intensity, is so great in "Autumnal Tints" that he needed thirty-three exclamation points and twenty-three words or phrases italicized for emphasis in the twenty-five page piece!

Most writers give us their best observations couched in their best language. Thoreau tries to go further, goading his reader to see more than has been described, and to express it even better than the writer could. After a detailed chronological account of what all is to be seen in a Concord autumn, he pauses to look back over what he has seen and to consider us, the readers, who are always his implied walking companions. "All this you surely *will* see, and much more, if you are prepared to see it, if you *look* for it" (Thoreau's emphasis). If you *actively* look for it, he means. At one point, speaking about the shape of a scarlet oak leaf, Thoreau says, "what a wild and pleasing outline, a combination of graceful curves and angles! The eye rests with equal delight on what is not leaf and on what is leaf."

By the time he came to work seriously on fall color, he knew how profoundly true it is that we see only what we are prepared to see. Early in January 1860, Thoreau observed in his journal:

A man receives only what he is ready to receive, whether physically or intellectually or morally, as animals conceive at certain seasons their kind only. We hear and apprehend only what we already half know. If there is something which does not concern me, which is out of my line, which by experience or by genius my attention is not drawn to, however novel and remarkable it may be, if it is spoken, we hear it not, if it is written, we read it not, or, if we read it, it does not detain us. Every man thus *tracks himself* through life, in all his hearing and reading and observation and traveling. The phenomenon or fact that cannot be in any wise linked with the rest which he has observed, he does not observe.[16]

Only if you are aware of how much you do not see, have you any chance of seeing something new. As John Ruskin put it in *Modern Painters*, a book Thoreau knew, in a passage singled out by Annie Dillard, "unless the minds of men are particularly directed to the impressions of sight, objects pass perpetually before the eyes without conveying any impression to the brain at all, and so pass actually unseen, not merely unnoticed, but in the full clear sense of the word, unseen."[17]

It is Henry Thoreau in the very essay before us who explains most clearly how to change all that. "Objects are concealed from our view, not so much because they are out of the course of our visual ray as because we do not bring our minds and eyes to bear on them; for there is no power to see in the eye itself, any more than in any other jelly." Everything depends on our volunteered, our willed attention, on our deliberate *intending* to see. Thoreau says, "there is just as much beauty visible to us in the landscape as we are prepared to appreciate—not a grain more." When John D. MacDonald's Travis McGee is running his houseboat, the *Busted Flush*, along close to the Florida shore, he passes a bar "where about forty pelicans stood in single file in about an inch of water." McGee points this out to his companion, a beautifully shaped but vapid woman named Vangie (for

Evangeline). She replies, "Yeah. Birds." McGee goes on, "Most people are as blind as Vangie. Eyesight is what you use to get around without running into things."[18]

The scarlet oak or the pelican "must, in a sense, be in your eye when you go forth," says Thoreau. "We cannot see anything until we are possessed with the idea of it, take it into our heads—and then we can hardly see anything else." The key to the kingdom of beauty is attention—separate and purposeful acts of intention. As early as his first book, *A Week on the Concord and Merrimack Rivers*, Thoreau could speak of how it required a "separate intention of the eye" to see each particular thing in the landscape, so in this, the last of his writings, he insists, "I have found that it required a different intention of the eye, in the same locality, to see different plants, even when they were closely allied."

We sometimes think of Henry Thoreau as an idler, a lazy saunterer, drifting blissfully and playing his flute through the Concord countryside without a care in the world. Thoreau himself encourages this view. But he was in fact a dedicated and carefully prepared observer who went on his afternoon walks with the equipment and purposefulness of an expedition leader. One of his walking companions noted, with a sort of dull incredulity, how Thoreau's notebook

> was never omitted, rain or shine. Abroad, he used the
> pencil, writing but a few moments at a time during

the walk, but into the notebook must go all measurements with the foot rule which he always carried, or the surveyor's tape that he often had with him. Also all observations with the spy-glass (another invariable companion) all conditions of plants, spring, summer, and fall, the depth of snows, the strangeness of the skies—all went down in his notebook. To his memory he never trusted for a fact, but to the page and the pencil and the abstract in the pocket, not the Journal.[19]

On a typical "ramble," actually more like an intensive nature walk, that of May 11, 1854, just to take a single random example, Thoreau saw, named, and logged in sixty-six different plants and fifteen different birds while describing a shower that left the grass many shades greener, the toads louder, and the walker himself more awake. Thoreau seems to have been like Sinclair Lewis's fictional scientist Martin Arrowsmith, whose great gift was the "curiosity by which he saw nothing as ordinary."

The world into which Thoreau walked was the world of plenitude described in Plato's *Timaeus*, a world as full as possible of as many different things as possible. It was the world of Darwin's tangled bank, a world of fascinated excitement over the vast but emphatically finite riches of the earth, which are far more interesting than the empty concept of the infinite. We speak easily of infinite space or infinite love, but we have not yet even listed or identified the obviously finite species of

fish in the Amazon. Fifteen to twenty thousand new species are discovered each year in the animal kingdom alone. It is estimated that only 15 percent of all the species on earth have been identified.[20] Instead of emphasizing the survival of the fittest or a nature red in tooth and claw, perhaps we should learn to think of the Darwinian world as a fantastic and still-challenging world of discoverable if not yet discovered richness and variety of species. Darwin left us with a richer, more specific world, not with a poorer one.

To see everything means, for Thoreau, to see every thing. The world into which he walked was also the pluralist world of Nicholas of Cusa, who held that "the precondition for the abundance of nature lies in what is restless, limited, change-able, and composite. Nothing living is one, it is always many." Even death, Cusanus thought, is "no more than the resolu-tion of a composite into its elements."[21] Like Zorba the Greek, Thoreau saw everything every day as though for the first time. We all walk out into the same multitudinous world, but who among us sees as much as Thoreau did? John Ruskin, from whom Thoreau learned so much about how to see, once said, "the worst of me is that the desire of my eyes is so much to me! Ever so much more than the desire of my mind."[22] On every walk, Thoreau threw himself into every observation with an ebullience rivaling Whitman's. "How beautiful, when a whole tree is like one great scarlet fruit full of ripe juices, every leaf, from lowest limb to topmost spire, all aglow, especially if you look toward the sun! What more remarkable object can there be in a landscape? Visible for miles, too fair to be believed. If such a phenomenon occurred but once, it would be handed down by tradition to posterity, and get into the mythology at last."

Your work should be the praise of what you love, said Ruskin, and nowhere does Thoreau give a better example of that than in this autumn piece. What you love is what you give your attention to, and Thoreau knew better than most that the key to noticing everything is the mental act of directed attention. Thoreau gives us the key to himself when he observes, "I have the habit of attention to such excess that my senses get no rest." If habit is "the structural unit of mental life," as Gordon Allport said of William James's work in *Psychology: Briefer Course*, it is also true, as James himself says, that "the whole drama of the voluntary life" hinges on the matter of attention, on the amount of directed attention we are able to muster. *Attention,* said James, is the same fact as *belief* and the same thing as *will.* James's friend Josiah Royce put it that "our own activity of attention will thus determine what we are to know and what we are to believe." Absolute attention is prayer, said Simone Weil. Thoreau would have understood.

It was Thoreau's ambition to see and record everything the natural world had on offer in Concord, and he died not only before he could do it but before he had to face the impossibility of doing it. This ambition is at the core of what Paul Rosenfeld called the "green American tradition." "Affirmation of man's whole nature, embrace of all the earth bound up with it . . . is the American principle," writes Rosenfeld. "If there is a green American tradition, this is it."[23]

As "Autumnal Tints" progresses, Thoreau's enthusiasm rises. "It is pleasant to walk over the beds of these fresh, crisp, and rustling leaves. How beautifully they go to their graves! How gently lay themselves down and turn to mould. . . . They teach us how to die."

How much Henry Thoreau can still deliver to us! Seen with such acuity and intensity of attention, the world might as well be emanationist, as so many different religions have proposed, that is, "an overflow or spontaneous expression of the divine." After all, as Goethe saw, "everything factual is already theory. The blueness of the sky reveals to us the basic laws of chromatics. One should seek nothing beyond phenomena; they themselves are the theory."[24]

Perhaps beauty has some Darwinian survival value here and there, but what in our everyday terrestrial lives explains or requires the astounding manifold beauty of the world? Is some earth-spirit or world-spirit trying to reach us with the only language it knows? Thoreau thought the autumn leaves were teaching us how to die. He himself died magnificently, at home, in bed, surrounded by family and friends. Mary Russell Watson—the Maiden in the East—"wrote constantly" to ask about his condition. When Ellen Sewall's name came up, he

said, "I have always loved her." Then he said it again. "I have always loved her."

His wit was the last thing to leave him. When an old friend, Parker Pillsbury, one of the abolitionist stalwarts, could not resist trying to peer into the future, he asked the dying Thoreau, "You seem so near the brink of the dark river, I almost wonder how the opposite shore may appear to you." Thoreau's answer summed up his life. "One world at a time," said he.

His death is our new life; now he belongs to us all. As the novelist Erich Maria Remarque observed, "the only beings we can possess entirely are the dead, because they cannot escape." Perhaps not, but they certainly can keep on asking questions. "The dead," said the historian Arno Borst, "can give no orders, they can't sue us to re-assert their sleeping [dormant] rights. It is our word alone that counts. But their silence asks: 'We played for you on the flute, we sang laments—did you hear nothing?'"[25]

—ROBERT D. RICHARDSON
April 9, 2011

NOTES

Details of Thoreau's life are taken from Walter Harding, *The Days of Henry Thoreau* (Princeton, NJ: Princeton University Press, 1982) and Robert D. Richardson, *Henry Thoreau: A Life of the Mind* (Berkeley, CA: University of California Press, 1986), unless otherwise noted. See also Shawn Stewart's excellent "Transcendental Romance Meets the Ministry of Pain: The Thoreau Brothers, Ellen Sewall, and Her Father" in *The Concord Saunterer*, new series, vol. 14 (2006).

1   Henry David Thoreau, *The Journal of Henry Thoreau*, ed. Bradford Torrey and Francis H. Allen (Boston: Houghton Mifflin, 1906; repr., Salt Lake City, UT: Peregrine Smith Books, 1984), September 24, 1859, vol. 12, p. 344.
2   Joel Myerson and Ronald Bosco, *The Emerson Brothers* (New York: Oxford University Press, 2006), p. 177.
3   Henry David Thoreau, *The Writings of Henry D. Thoreau, Journal*, vol. 1, *1837–1844* (Princeton, NJ: Princeton University Press, 1981), pp. 316, 324.
4   Ibid., pp. 316–17.
5   Ibid., p. 347.
6   Ralph Waldo Emerson, *The Journals and Miscellaneous Notebooks of Ralph Waldo Emerson*, ed. William H. Gilman et al. (Cambridge, MA: Harvard University Press, 1973), vol. 8, p. 164n.
7   Ibid., p. 165.
8   Henry David Thoreau, *The Correspondence of Henry Thoreau*, ed. Walter Harding and Carl Bode (New York: New York University Press, 1958), p. 62.
9   Henry W. Longfellow, *Kavanagh* (Boston: Ticknor, Reed and Fields, 1849), book 1, chap. 1.
10 Thoreau, *Writings*, vol. 1, p. 368.
11 Thoreau, *Correspondence*, pp. 64-65.

12 Ralph Waldo Emerson, *The Letters of Ralph Waldo Emerson*, ed. R. L. Rusk (New York: Columbia University Press, 1939), vol. 3, p. 8.

13 Thoreau, *Correspondence*, p. 67.

14 Thoreau, *Writings*, vol. 1, p. 374.

15 Robert F. Clarke, "Thoreau's Last Lecture," *Thoreau Society Bulletin*, no. 266 (Spring 2009), pp. 1–5.

16 Thoreau, *Journal*, January 5, 1860, vol. 12, p. 77.

17 John Ruskin, *Modern Painters*, 3rd ed. (New York: John Wiley and Sons, 1880), part 2, sec. 1, chap. 2, p. 51.

18 John D. MacDonald, *Darker than Amber* (New York: Fawcett, 1987), pp. 47–48.

19 Ellery Channing, *Thoreau the Poet-Naturalist* (Boston: Roberts Brothers, 1873), pp. 65–66; Thoreau, *Writings*, vol. 1, p. 615.

20 Natalie Angier, "New Creatures in an Age of Extinction," *New York Times*, July 26, 2009, pp. 1, 3.

21 Anita Albus, *The Art of Arts: Rediscovering Painting* (Berkeley, CA: University of California Press, 2001), p. 40.

22 Wolfgang Kemp, *The Desire of My Eyes: The Life and Work of John Ruskin* (New York: Farrar, Straus and Giroux, 1992), p. 450.

23 Paul Rosenfeld, *By Way of Art: Criticisms of Music, Literature, Painting, Sculpture, and the Dance* (New York: Coward-McCann, 1928), p. 302.

24 Quoted by Albus in *Art of Arts*, p. 99.

25 Ibid., p. 271.

Autumnal Tints

Europeans coming to America are surprised by the brilliancy of our autumnal foliage. There is no account of such a phenomenon in English poetry, because the trees acquire but few bright colors there. The most that Thompson says on this subject in his "Autumn" is contained in the lines—

> "But see the fading many-colored woods,
> Shade deepening over shade, the country round
> Imbrown; a crowded umbrage, dusk and dun,
> Of every hue, from wan-declining green
> To sooty dark."—

And the line in which he speaks of

> "Autumn beaming o'er the yellow woods."

The autumnal change of our woods has not made a deep impression on our own literature yet. October has hardly tinged our poetry.

A great many, who have spent their lives in cities, and have never chanced to come into the country at this season, have never seen this the flower, or rather ripe fruit, of the year. I remember riding with one such citizen, who, though a fortnight too late for the most brilliant tints, was taken by surprise, and would not believe that there had been any brighter. He had never heard of this phenomenon before. Not only many in our towns have never witnessed it, but it is scarcely remembered by the majority from year to year.

Most appear to confound changed leaves with withered ones, as if they were to confound ripe apples with rotten ones. I think that the change to some higher color in a leaf is an evidence that it has arrived at a late and perfect maturity, answering to the maturity of fruits. It is generally the lowest and oldest leaves which change first. But as the perfect winged and usually bright-colored insect is short-lived, so the leaves ripen but to fall.

Generally, every fruit, on ripening, and just before it falls, when it commences a more independent and individual existence, requiring less nourishment from any source, and that not so much from the earth through its stem as from the sun and air, acquires a bright tint. So do leaves. The physiologist says it is "due to an increased absorption of oxygen." That is the scientific account of the matter,—only a reassertion of the fact. But I am more interested in the rosy cheek than I am to know what particular diet the maiden fed on. The very forest and herbage, the pellicle of the earth, must acquire a bright color, an evidence of its ripeness,—as if the glove itself were a fruit on its stem, with ever a cheek toward the sun.

Flowers are but colored leaves, fruits but ripe ones. The edible part of most fruits is, as the physiologist says, "the parenchyma or fleshy tissue of the leaf" of which they are formed.

Our appetites have commonly confined our views of ripeness and its phenomena, color, mellowness, and perfectness, to the fruits which we eat, and we are wont to forget that an immense harvest which we do not eat, hardly use at all, is annually ripened by Nature. At our annual Cattle Shows and Horticultural Exhibitions, we make, as we think, a great show of fair fruits, destined, however, to a rather ignoble end, fruits not valued for their beauty chiefly. But round about and within our towns there is annually another show of fruits, on an infinitely grander scale, fruits which address our taste for beauty alone.

October is the month of painted leaves. Their rich glow now flashes round the world. As fruits and leaves and the day itself acquire a bright tint, just before they fall, so the year near its setting. October is its sunset sky; November the later twilight.

I formerly thought that it would be worth the while to get a specimen leaf from each changing tree, shrub and herbaceous plant, when it had acquired its brightest characteristic color, in its transition from the green to the brown state, outline it and copy its color exactly with paint in a book, which should be entitled October, or Autumnal Tints. Beginning with the earliest reddening—woodbine and the lake of radical leaves, and coming down through the maples, hickories and sumacs, and many beautifully freckled leaves less generally known, to the latest oaks and aspens. What a memento such a book would be! You would need only to turn over its leaves to take a ramble through the Autumn woods whenever you pleased. Or if I could preserve the leaves themselves unfaded, it would be better still. I have made but little progress toward such a book, but I have endeavored instead to describe all these bright tints in the order in which they present themselves. The following are some extracts from my notes.

THE PURPLE GRASSES

By the twentieth of August, everywhere in woods and swamps, we are reminded of the fall, both by the richly spotted Sarsaparilla-leaves and Brakes, and the withering and blackened Skunk-Cabbage and Hellebore, and, by the riverside, the already blackening Pontederia.

The Purple Grass (*Eragrostis pectinacea*) is now in the height of its beauty. I remember still when I first noticed this grass particularly. Standing on a hill-side near our river, I saw, thirty or forty rods off, a stripe of purple half a dozen rods long, under the edge of a wood, where the ground sloped toward a meadow. It was as high-colored and interesting, though not quite so bright, as the patches of Rhexia, being a darker purple, like a berry's stain laid on close and thick. On going to and examin-

ing it, I found it to be a kind of grass in bloom, hardly a foot
high, with but few green blades, and a fine spreading panicle
of purple flowers, a shallow, purplish mist trembling around
me. Close at hand it appeared but a dull purple, and made little
impression on the eye. It was even difficult to detect, and if
you plucked a single plant you were surprised to find how thin
it was, and how little color it had. But viewed at a distance
in a favorable light, it was of a fine lively purple, flower-like,
enriching the earth. Such puny causes combine to produce
these decided effects. I was the more surprised and charmed
because grass is commonly of a sober and humble color.

With its beautiful purple blush it reminds me and supplies
the place of the rhexia which is now leaving off, and it is one of
the most interesting phenomena of August. The finest patches
of it grow on waste strips or selvedges of land at the base of
dry hills, just above the edge of the meadows, where the greedy
mower does not deign to swing his scythe; for this is a thin
and poor grass, beneath his notice. Or, it may be, because it is
so beautiful he does not know that it exists; for the same eye
does not see this and timothy. He carefully gets the meadow
hay and the more nutritious grasses which grow next to that,
but he leaves this fine purple mist for the walker's harvest—
fodder for his fancy stock. Higher up the hill perchance grow
also black-berries, johnswort and neglected, withered and wiry
June-grass. How fortunate that it grows in such places and not
in the midst of the rank grasses which are annually cut! Nature

thus keeps use and beauty distinct. I know many such localities where it does not fail to present itself annually and paint the earth with its blush. It grows either in a continuous patch, or in scattered and rounded tufts a foot in diameter on the gentle slopes, and it lasts till it is killed by the first smart frosts.

In most plants the corolla or calyx is the part which attains the highest color, and is the most attractive; in many it is the seed-vessel or fruit; in others, as the Red Maple, the leaves; and in others still it is the very culm itself which is the principal flower or blooming part.

The last is especially the case with the Poke or Garget (*Phytolacca decandra*). Some which stand under our cliffs quite dazzle me with their purple stems now and early in September. They are as interesting to me as most flowers, and one of the most important fruits of our autumn. Every part is flower, (or fruit,) such is its superfluity of color,—stem, branch, peduncle, pedicel, petiole, and even the at length yellowish purple-veined leaves. Its cylindrical racemes of berries of various hues, from green to dark purple, six or seven inches long, are gracefully drooping on all sides, offering repasts to the birds; and even the sepals from which the birds have picked the berries are a brilliant lake-red, with crimson flame-like reflections, equal to anything of the kind,—all on fire with ripeness. Hence the *lacca*, from *lac*, lake. There are at the same time flower-buds, flowers, green berries, dark purple or ripe ones, and these flower-like sepals, all on the same plant.

We love to see any redness in the vegetation of the temperate zone. It is the color of colors. This plant speaks to our blood. It asks a bright sun on it to make it show to best advantage, and it must be seen at this season of the year. On warm hill-sides its stems are ripe by the twenty-third of August. At that date I walked through a beautiful grove of them, six or seven feet high, on the side of one of our cliffs, where they ripen early. Quite to the ground they were a deep brilliant purple with a bloom, contrasting with the still clear green leaves. It appears a rare triumph of Nature to have produced and perfected such a plant, as if this were enough for a summer. What a perfect maturity it arrives at! It is the emblem of a successful life, concluded by a death not premature, which is an ornament to nature. What if we were to mature as perfectly, root and branch, glowing in the midst of our decay, like the Poke! I confess, that it excites me to behold them. I cut one for a cane, for I would fain handle and lean on it. I love to press the berries between my fingers, and see their juice staining my hand. To walk amid these upright branching casks of purple wine, which retain and diffuse a sunset glow, tasting each one with your eye, instead of counting the pipes on a London dock, what a privilege! For Nature's vintage is not confined to the vine. Our poets have sung of wine, the product of a foreign plant which commonly they never saw, as if our own plants had no juice in them more than the singers. Indeed, this has been called by some the American Grape, and, though a native of America, its juices are used in some foreign countries to improve the color of the wine; so that the poetaster may be celebrating the virtues of the Poke without knowing it. Here are berries enough to paint afresh the western sky, and play the bacchanal with, if you will. And what flutes its ensanguined stems would make, to be used in such a dance! It is truly a royal plant. I could spend the evening of the year musing amid the Pokestems. And perchance amid these groves might arise at last a new school of philosophy or poetry. It lasts all through September.

At the same time with this, or near the end of August, a to me very interesting genus of grasses, Andropogons, or Beard-Grasses, is in its prime. *Andropogon furcatus*, Forked Beard-Grass, or call it Purple-Fingered Grass; *Andropogon scoparius*, Purple Wood-Grass; and *Andropogon* (now called *Sorghum*) *nutans*, Indian-Grass. The first is a very tall and slender-culmed grass, three to seven feet high, with four or five purple finger-like spikes raying upward from the top. The second is also quite slender, growing in tufts two feet high by one wide, with culms often somewhat curving, which, as the spikes go out of bloom, have a whitish fuzzy look. These two are prevailing grasses at this season on dry and sandy fields and hill-sides. The culms of both, not to mention their pretty flowers, reflect a purple tinge, and help to declare the ripeness of the year. Perhaps I have the more sympathy with them because they are despised by the farmer, and occupy sterile and neglected soil. They are high-colored, like ripe grapes, and express a maturity which the spring did not suggest. Only the August sun could have thus burnished these culms and leaves. The farmer has long since done his upland haying, and he will not condescend to bring his scythe to where these slender wild grasses have at length flowered thinly; you often see spaces of bare sand amid them. But I walk encouraged between the tufts of Purple Wood-Grass, over the sandy fields, and along the edge of the Shrub-Oaks, glad to recognize these simple contemporaries. With thoughts cutting a broad swathe I "get" them, with horse-raking thoughts I gather them into windrows. The fine-eared poet may hear the whetting of my scythe. These two were almost the first grasses that I learned to distinguish, for I had not known by how many friends I was surrounded,—I had seen them simply as grasses standing. The purple of their culms also excites me like that of the Poke-Weed stems.

Think what refuge there is for one, before August is over, from college commencements and society that isolates! I can skulk amid the tufts of Purple Wood-Grass on the borders of the "Great Fields." Wherever I walk these afternoons, the Purple-Fingered Grass also stands like a guide-board, and points my thoughts to more poetic paths than they have lately travelled.

A man shall perhaps rush by and trample down plants as high as his head, and cannot be said to know that they exist, though he may have cut many tons of them, littered his stables with them, and fed them to his cattle for years. Yet, if he ever favorably attends to them, he may be overcome by their beauty. Each humblest plant, or weed, as we call it, stands there to express some thought or mood of ours; and yet how long it stands in vain! I had walked over those Great Fields so many Augusts, and never yet distinctly recognized these purple companions that I had there. I had brushed against them and trodden on them, forsooth; and now, at last, they, as it were, rose up and blessed me. Beauty and true wealth are always thus cheap and despised. Heaven might be defined as the place which men avoid. Who can doubt that these grasses, which the farmer says are of no account to him, find some compensation in your appreciation of them? I may say that I never saw them before,—though, when I came to look them face to face, there did come down to me a purple gleam from previous years; and now, wherever I go, I see hardly anything else. It is the reign and presidency of the Andropogons.

Almost the very sands confess the ripening influence of the August sun, and methinks, together with the slender grasses waving over them, reflect a purple tinge. The impurpled sands! Such is the consequence of all this sunshine absorbed into the pores of plants and of the earth. All sap or blood is now wine-colored. At last we have not only the purple sea, but the purple land.

The Chestnut Beard-Grass, Indian-Grass, or Wood-Grass, growing here and there in waste places, but more rare than the former, (from two to four or five feet high,) is still handsomer and of more vivid colors than its congeners, and might well have caught the Indian's eye. It has a long, narrow, one-sided, and slightly nodding panicle of bright purple and yellow flowers, like a banner raised above its reedy leaves. These bright standards are now advanced on the distant hill-sides, not in large armies, but in scattered troops or single file, like the red men. They stand thus fair and bright, representative of the race which they are named after, but for the most part unobserved as they. The expression of this grass haunted me for a week, after I first passed and noticed it, like the glance of an eye. It stands like an Indian chief taking a last look at his favorite hunting-grounds.

THE RED MAPLE

By the 25th of September, the Red Maples generally are *beginning* to be ripe. Some large ones have been conspicuously changing for a week, and some single trees are now very brilliant. I notice a small one, half a mile off across a meadow, against the green wood-side there, a far brighter red than the blossoms of any tree in summer, and more conspicuous. I have observed this tree for several autumns invariably changing earlier than its fellows, just as one tree ripens its fruit earlier than another. It might serve to mark the season perhaps. I should be sorry if it were cut down. I know of 2 or 3 such trees in different parts of my town, which might perhaps be propagated from as early ripeners or September trees, and their seed be advertised in

the market, as well as that of radishes, if we cared as much about them.

At present, these burning bushes stand chiefly along the edge of the meadows, or I distinguish them afar on the hill-sides here and there. Sometimes you will see many small ones in a swamp turned quite crimson when all other trees around are still perfectly green, and the former appear so much the brighter for it. They take you by surprise as you are going by on one side, across the fields, thus early in the season, as if it were some gay encampment of the redmen, or other foresters, of whose arrival you had not heard.

Some single trees, wholly bright scarlet, seen against others of their kind still freshly green, or against evergreens, are more memorable than whole groves will be by and by. How beautiful when a whole tree is like one great scarlet fruit, full of ripe juices, every leaf, from lowest limb to topmost spire, all a-glow, especially if you look toward the sun. What more remarkable object can there be in the landscape? Visible for miles, too fair to be believed. If such a phenomenon occurred but once, it would be handed down by tradition to posterity, and get into the mythology at last.

The whole tree thus ripening in advance of its fellows attains a singular preeminence, and sometimes maintains it for a week or two. I am thrilled at the sight of it, bearing aloft its scarlet standard for the regiment of green-clad foresters around, and I go half a mile out of my way to examine it. A single tree becomes thus the crowning beauty of some meadowy vale, and the expression of the whole surrounding forest is at once more spirited for it.

A small Red Maple has grown, perchance, far away at the head of some retired valley, a mile from any road, unobserved. It has faithfully discharged the duties of a Maple there, all winter and summer, neglected none of its economies, but added to its stature in the virtue which belongs to a Maple, by a steady growth for so many months, never having gone gadding abroad, and is nearer heaven than it was in the spring. It has faithfully husbanded its sap, and afforded a shelter to the wandering bird, has long since ripened its seeds and committed them to the winds, and has the satisfaction of knowing, perhaps, that a thousand little well-behaved Maples are already settled in life somewhere. It deserves well of Mapledom. Its leaves have been asking it from time to time, in a whisper, "When shall we redden?" And now, in this month of September, this month of traveling, when men are hastening to the sea-side, or the mountains, or the lakes, this modest Maple, still without budging an inch, travels in its reputation,—runs up its scarlet flag on that hill-side, which shows that it has finished its summer's work before all other trees, and withdraws from the contest. At the eleventh hour of the year, the tree which no scrutiny could have detected here when it was most industrious is thus, by the tint of its maturity, by its very blushes, revealed at last to the careless and distant traveller, and leads his thoughts away from the dusty road into those brave solitudes which it inhabits. It flashes out conspicuous with all the virtue and beauty of a Maple,—*Acer rubrum*. We may now read its title, or *rubric*, clear. Its *virtues*, not its sins, are as scarlet.

Notwithstanding that the Red Maple is the most intense scarlet of any of our trees, the Sugar Maple has been the most celebrated, and Michaux, in his Sylva does not speak of the autumnal color of the former. About the 2nd of October these trees, both large and small, are most brilliant, though many are still green. In sprout-lands they seem to vie with one another, and ever some particular one in the midst of the crowd will be of a peculiarly pure scarlet, and by its more intense color attract our eye even at a distance, and carry off the palm. A large Red Maple swamp, when at the height of its change, is the most obviously brilliant of all tangible things, where I dwell, so abundant is this tree with us. It varies much both in form and color. A great many are merely yellow, more Scarlet, others scarlet deepening into crimson, more red than common. Look at yonder swamp of Maples mixed with Pines, at the base of a pine-clad hill, a quarter of a mile off, so that you get the full effect of the bright colors, without detecting the imperfections of the leaves and see their yellow, scarlet and crimson fires, of all tints, mingled and contrasted with the green.

Some Maples are yet green, only yellow or crimson-tipt on the edges of their flakes, as the edges of a hazelnut burr, some are wholly brilliant scarlet, raying out regularly and finely every way, bilaterally, like the veins of a leaf; others, of more irregular form, when I turn my head slightly, emptying out some of its earthiness and concealing the trunk of the tree, seem to rest heavily flake on flake like yellow and scarlet clouds, wreath upon wreath, or like snow drifts driving through the air, stratified by the wind. It adds greatly to the beauty of such a swamp at this season, that, even though there may be no other trees interspersed, it is not seen as a simple mass of color, but different trees being of different colors and hues the outline of each crescent tree top is distinct, and where one laps onto another. Yet a painter would hardly venture to make them thus distinct a quarter of a mile off.

As I go across a meadow directly towards a low rising ground this bright afternoon, I see, some fifty rods off toward the sun the top of a Maple swamp just appearing over the sheeny russet edge of the hill, a stripe apparently twenty rods long by ten feet deep, of the most intensely brilliant scarlet, orange and yellow equal to any flowers or fruits, or any tints ever painted. As I advance, lowering the edge of the hill which makes the firm foreground or lower frame of the picture, the depth of the brilliant grove revealed steadily increases, suggesting that the whole of the enclosed valley is filled with such color. One wonders that the tithing men and fathers of the town are not out to see what the trees mean by their high colors and exuberance of spirits, fearing that some mischief is brewing. I do not see what the Puritans did at this season when the maples

blaze out in scarlet. They certainly could not have worshipped in groves then. Perhaps that is what they built meeting houses and fenced them round with horse-sheds for.

THE ELM

Now, too, the first of October, or later, the Elms are at the height of their autumnal beauty, great brownish-yellow masses, warm from their September oven, hanging over the highway. Their leaves are perfectly ripe. I wonder if there is any answering ripeness in the lives of the men who live beneath them. As I look down our street, which is lined with them, they remind me both by their form and color of yellowing sheaves of grain, as if the harvest had indeed come to the village itself, and we might expect to find some maturity and *flavor* in the thoughts of the villagers at last. Under those bright rustling yellow piles just ready to fall on the heads of the walkers, how can any crudity or greenness of thought or act prevail? When I stand where half a dozen large Elms droop over a house, it is as if I stood within a ripe pumpkin-rind, and I feel as mellow as if I were the pulp, though I may be somewhat stringy and seedy withal. What is the late greenness of the English Elm, like a cucumber out of season, which does not know when to have done, compared with the early and golden maturity of the American tree? The street is the scene of a great harvest-home. It would be worth the while to set out these trees, if only for their autumnal value. Think of these great yellow canopies or parasols held over our heads and houses by the mile together, making the village all one and compact,—an *ulmarium*, which is at the same time a nursery of men! And then how gently and unobserved they drop their burden and let in the sun when it is wanted, their leaves not heard when they fall on our roofs and in our streets; and thus the village parasol is shut up and put away! I see the market-man driving into the village, and disappearing under its canopy of Elm-tops, with *his* crop, as into a great granary or barn-yard. I am tempted to go thither as to a husking of thoughts, now dry and ripe and ready to be separated from their integuments; but alas! I foresee that it will be chiefly husks and little thought, blasted pig-corn, fit only for cob-meal—for as you sow so shall you reap.

FALLEN LEAVES

By the sixth of October the leaves generally begin to fall, in successive showers, after frost or rain; but the principal leaf-harvest, the acme of the *Fall*, is commonly about the sixteenth. Some morning at that date there is perhaps a harder frost than we have seen, and ice formed under the pump, and now, when the morning wind rises, the leaves come down in denser showers than ever. They suddenly form thick beds or carpets on the ground, in this gentle air, or even without wind, just the size and form of the tree above. Some trees, as small Hickories, appear to have dropped their leaves instantaneously, as a soldier grounds arms at a signal; and those of the Hickory,

being bright yellow still, though withered, reflect a blaze of light from the ground where they lie. Down they have come on all sides, at the first earnest touch of autumn's wand, making a sound like rain.

Or else it is after moist and rainy weather that we notice how great a fall of leaves there has been in the night, though it may not yet be the touch that loosens the Rock-Maple leaf. The streets are thickly strewn with the trophies, and fallen Elm-leaves make a dark brown pavement under our feet. After some remarkably warm Indian-summer day or days, I perceive that it is the unusual heat which, more than anything, causes the leaves to fall, there having been, perhaps, no frost nor rain for some time. The intense heat suddenly ripens and wilts them, just as it softens and ripens peaches and other fruits, and causes them to drop.

The leaves of late Red Maples, still bright, strew the earth, often crimson-spotted on a yellow ground, like some wild apples,—though they preserve these bright colors on the ground but a day or two, especially if it rains. On causeways I go by trees here and there all bare and smoke-like, having lost their brilliant clothing; but there it lies, nearly as bright as ever, on the ground on one side, and making nearly as regular a figure as lately on the tree. I would rather say that I first observe the trees thus flat on the ground like a permanent colored shadow, and they suggest to look for the boughs that bore them. A queen might be proud to walk where these gallant trees have spread their bright cloaks in the mud. I see wagons roll over them as a shadow or a reflection, and the drivers heed them just as little as they did their shadows before.

Birds'-nests, in the Huckleberry and other shrubs, and in trees, are already being filled with the withered leaves. So many have fallen in the woods, that a squirrel cannot run after a falling nut without being heard. Boys are raking them in the streets, if only for the pleasure of dealing with such clean crisp substances. Some sweep the paths scrupulously neat, and then stand to see the next breath strew them with new trophies. The swamp-floor is thickly covered, and the *Lycopodium lucidulum* looks suddenly greener amid them. In dense woods they half-cover pools that are three or four rods long. The other day I could hardly find a well-known spring, and even suspected that it had dried up, for it was completely concealed by freshly fallen leaves; and when I swept them aside and revealed it, it was like striking the earth, with Aaron's rod, for a new spring. Wet grounds about the edges of swamps look dry with them. At one swamp, where I was surveying, thinking to step on a leafy shore from a rail, I got into the water more than a foot deep.

When I go to the river the day after the principal fall of leaves, the sixteenth, I find my boat all covered, bottom and seats, with the leaves of the Golden Willow, under which it is moored, and I set sail with a cargo of them rustling under my feet. If I empty it it will be full again tomorrow. I do not regard them as litter to be swept out, but accept them as suit-

able straw or matting for the bottom of my carriage. When I turn up into the mouth of the Assabet, which is wooded, large fleets of leaves are floating on its surface, as it were getting out to sea, with room to tack, but next the shore, a little further up, they are thicker than foam, quite concealing the water for a rod in width, under and amid the Alders, Button-bushes and Maples, still perfectly light and dry with fiber unrelaxed; and at a rocky bend, where they are met and stopped by the morning wind, they sometimes form a broad and dense crescent, quite across the river. When I turn my prow that way and the wave which it makes strikes them, list what a pleasant rustling from these dry substances, grating on one another. Often it is their undulation only which reveals the water beneath them. Also every motion of the wood turtle on the shore is betrayed by their rustling there. Or even in mid channel, when the wind rises, I hear them blown with a rustling sound. Higher up they are slowly moving round and round in some great eddy which the river makes, as that at the "Leaning Hemlocks", where the water is deep, and the current is wearing into the bank.

Perchance, in the afternoon of such a day, when the water is perfectly calm and full of reflections, I paddle gently down the main stream, and turning up the Assabet reach a quiet cove where I unexpectedly find myself surrounded by myriads of leaves like fellow voyagers which seem to have the same purpose or want of purpose, with myself. See this great fleet of scattered leaf-boats which we paddle amid, in this smooth river bay, each one curled up on every side by the sun's skill; each nerve a stiff Spruce knee; like boats of hide and of all patterns, Charon's boat probably among the rest, and some with lofty prows and poops like the stately vessels of the ancients, scarcely moving in the sluggish current,—like the great fleets, the dense Chinese cities, of boats, with which you mingle on entering some great mart, some New York or Canton, which we are all steadily approaching together.

How gently each has been deposited on the water. No violence has been used towards them yet, though perchance palpitating hearts were present at the launching. And painted ducks too, the splendid Wood-duck, among the rest, often come to sail and float amid the painted leaves—barks of a nobler model still!

What wholesome herb drinks are to be had in the swamps now! What strong medicinal but rich scents from the decaying leaves! The rain falling on the freshly dried herbs and leaves, and filling the pools and ditches into which they have dropped thus clean and rigid, will soon convert them into tea—green, black, brown and yellow teas, of all degrees of strength, enough to set all Nature a-gossiping. Whether we drink them or not, as yet, before their strength is drawn, these leaves, dried on Great Nature's coppers, are of such various pure and delicate tints as might make the fame of oriental teas.

How they are mixed up, of all species, Oak, and Maple, and Chestnut, and Birch. But Nature is not cluttered with them. She is a perfect husbandman; she stores them all. Consider what a vast crop is thus annually shed on the earth! This more than any mere grain or seed is the great harvest of the year. The trees are now repaying the earth with interest—what they have taken from it. They are discounting. They are about to add a leaf's thickness to the depth of the soil. This is the beautiful way in which Nature gets her muck, while I chaffer with this man and that, who talks to me about sulphur and the cost of carting. We are all the richer for their decay. I am more interested in this crop than in the English grass alone or in the corn. It prepares the virgin mould for future cornfields and forests, on which the earth fattens. It keeps our homestead in good heart.

For beautiful variety no crop can be compared with this. Here is not merely the plain yellow of the grains, but nearly all the colors that we know, the brightest blue not excepted. The early blushing Maple, the poison Sumac blazing its sins as scarlet, the mulberry Ash, the rich chrome yellow of the Poplars, the brilliant red Huckleberry, with which the hills' backs are painted, like those of sheep. The frost touches them, and with the slightest breath of returning day or jarring of earth's axle, see in what showers they come floating down. The ground is all particolored with them. But they still live in the soil whose fertility and bulk they increase, and in the forests that spring from it. They stoop to rise, to mount higher in coming years, by subtle chemistry, climbing by the sap in the trees, and the sapling's first fruits thus shed, transmuted at last, may adorn its crown, when in after years, it has become the monarch of the forest.

It is pleasant to walk over the beds of these fresh, crisp, and rustling leaves. How beautifully they go to their graves! how gently lay themselves down and turn to mould!—painted of a thousand hues, and fit to make the beds of us living. So they troop to their last resting-place, light and frisky. They put on no weeds, but merrily they go scampering over the earth, selecting the spot, choosing a lot, ordering no iron fence, whispering all through the woods about it,—some choosing the spot where the bodies of men are mouldering beneath, and meeting them half-way. How many flutterings before they rest quietly in their graves! They that soared so loftily, how contentedly they return to dust again, and are laid low, resigned to lie and decay at the foot of the tree, and afford nourishment to new generations of their kind, as well as to flutter on high! They teach us how to die. One wonders if the time will ever come when men, with their boasted faith in immortality, will lie down as gracefully and as ripe,—with such an Indian-summer serenity will shed their bodies, as they do their hair and nails.

When the leaves fall, the whole earth is a cemetery pleasant to walk in. I love to wander and muse over them in their graves. Here are no lying nor vain epitaphs. What though you own no lot at Mount Auburn? Your lot is surely cast somewhere in this vast cemetery, which has been consecrated from of old. You need attend no auction to secure a place. There is room enough here. The Loose-strife shall bloom and the Huckleberry-bird sing over your bones. The woodman and hunter shall be your

sextons, and the children shall tread upon the borders as much as they will. Let us walk in the cemetery of the leaves,—this is your true Greenwood Cemetery.

THE SUGAR MAPLE

But think not that the splendor of the year is over, for if one leaf does not make a summer neither does one fallen leaf make an Autumn. The smallest Sugar Maples in our streets make a great show as early as the fifth of October, more than any trees there. As I look up the Main Street they appear like painted screens standing before the houses, yet many are green. But now, or generally by the 17th of October, when almost all Red Maples, and some White Maples are bare, the large Sugar Maples also are in their glory, glowing with yellow and red and show unexpectedly bright and delicate tints. They are remarkable for the contrast they often afford of deep blushing red on one half, and green on the other. They become at length dense masses of rich yellow with a deep scarlet blush, or more than blush, on the exposed surfaces. They are the brightest trees now in the street.

The large ones on our common are particularly beautiful. A delicate, but warmer than golden yellow is now the prevailing color, with scarlet cheeks. Yet standing on the east side of the Common just before sundown, when the western light is transmitted through them, I see that their yellow even, compared with the pale lemon yellow of an Elm close by, amounts to a scarlet, without noticing the bright scarlet portions. Generally, they are great regular oval masses of yellow and scarlet. All the sunny warmth of the season, the Indian summer, seems to be absorbed in their leaves. The lowest and inmost leaves next the bole are, as usual, of the most delicate yellow and green, like the complexion of young men brought up in the house. There is an auction on the Common to-day, but its red flag is hard to be discerned amid this blaze of color.

Little did the fathers of the town anticipate this brilliant success, when they caused to be imported from further in the country some straight poles with their tops cut off, which they called Sugar-Maples; and, as I remember, after they were set out, a neighboring merchant's clerk, by way of jest, planted beans about them. Those which were then jestingly called beanpoles are to-day far the most beautiful objects noticeable in our streets. They are worth all and more than they have cost,—though one of the selectmen, while setting them out, took the cold which occasioned his death,—if only because they have filled the open eyes of children with their rich color unstintedly so many Octobers. We will not ask them to yield us sugar in the spring, while they afford us so fair a prospect in the autumn. Wealth in-doors may be the inheritance of few, but it is equally distributed on the Common. All children alike can revel in this golden harvest.

Surely trees should be set in our streets with a view to their October splendor; though I doubt whether this is ever consid-

ered by the "Tree Society." Do you not think it will make some
odds to these children that they were brought up under the
Maples? Hundreds of eyes are steadily drinking in this color,
and by these teachers even the truants are caught and educated
the moment they step abroad. Indeed, neither the truant nor the
studious are at present taught colors in the schools. These are
instead of the bright colors in apothecaries' shops and city windows. It is a pity that we have no more *Red* Maples, and some
Hickories, in our streets as well. Our paint-box is very imper-
fectly filled. Instead of, or beside, supplying such paint-boxes
as we do, we might supply these natural colors to the young.
Where else will they study color under greater advantages?
What School of Design can vie with this? Think how much
the eyes of painters of all kinds, and of manufacturers of cloth
and paper, and paper-stainers, and countless others, are to be
educated by these autumnal colors. The stationer's envelopes
may be of very various tints, yet not so various as those of the
leaves of a single tree. If you want a different shade or tint of a
particular color, you have only to look further within or without
the tree or the wood. These leaves are not many dipped in one
dye, as at the dye-house, but they are dyed in light of infinitely
various degrees of strength, and left to set and dry there.

Shall the names of so many of our colors continue to be
derived from those of obscure foreign localities, as Naples
yellow, Prussian blue, raw Sienna, burnt Umber, Gamboge?—
(surely the Tyrian purple must have faded by this time)—or

from comparatively trivial articles of commerce,—chocolate, lemon, coffee, cinnamon, claret?—(shall we compare our Hickory to a lemon, or a lemon to a Hickory?)—or from ores and oxides which few ever see? Shall we so often, when describing to our neighbors the color of something we have seen, refer them, not to some natural object in our neighborhood, but perchance to a bit of earth fetched from the other side of the planet, which possibly they may find at the apothecary's, but which probably neither they nor we ever saw? Have we not an *earth* under our feet,—ay, and a sky over our heads? Or is the last *all* ultramarine? What do we know of sapphire, amethyst, emerald, ruby, amber, and the like,—most of us who take these names in vain? Leave these precious words to cabinet keepers, virtuosos and maids of honor, to the Nabobs, Begums and Chobdars of Hindostan,—or wherever else. I do not see why, since America and her autumn woods have been discovered, our leaves should not compete with the precious stones in giving names to colors, and, indeed, I believe that in course of time, the names of some of our trees and shrubs as well as flowers will get into our popular chromatic nomenclature.

But of much more importance than a knowledge of the names and distinctions of color, is the joy and exhilaration which these colored leaves excite. Already these brilliant trees throughout the street, without any more variety, are at least equal to an annual festival and holiday, or a week of such. These are cheap and innocent galadays, celebrated by one and all without the

aid of committees or marshals, such a show as may safely be
licensed, not attracting gamblers nor rum-sellers, nor requiring
any special police to keep the peace; and poor indeed must be
that New England village's October which has not the Maple
in its streets. This October festival costs no powder, nor ring-
ing of bells, but every tree is a living liberty pole on which a
thousand bright flags are waving.

No wonder that we must have our annual cattle-show, and
Fall Training, and perhaps Cornwallis—our September Courts,
and the like—Nature herself holds her annual Fair in October,
not only in the streets, but in every hollow and on every hill
side. When lately we looked into that Red Maple swamp all
a-blaze, where the trees were clothed in their vestures of most
dazzling tints, did it not suggest a thousand Gypsies beneath—
a race capable of wild delight—or even the fabled fawns, satyrs
and wood-nymphs come back to earth? Or was it only a con-
gregation of wearied wood choppers, or of proprietors come to
inspect their lots, that we thought of? Or, earlier still, when we
paddled on the river through that fine-grained September air,
did there not appear to be something new going on under the
sparkling surface of the stream, a shaking of props, at least, so
that we made haste in order to be up in time? Did not the rows
of yellowing willows and button-bushes on each side seem like
rows of booths under which perhaps some fluviatile egg-pop
equally yellow was effervescing? —Did not all these suggest
that man's spirits should rise as high as Nature's—should hang

out their flag, and the routine of his life be interrupted by an analogous expression of joy and hilarity?

No annual training or muster of soldiery, no celebration with its scarfs and banners, could import into the town a hundredth part of the annual splendor of our October. We have only to set the trees, or let them stand, and Nature will find the colored drapery,—flags of all her nations, some of whose private signals hardly the botanist can read,—while we walk under the triumphal arches of the Elms. Leave it to Nature to appoint the days, whether the same as in neighboring States or not, and let the clergy read her proclamations, if they can understand them. Behold what a brilliant drapery is her Woodbine flag! What public-spirited merchant, think you, has contributed this part of the show? There is no handsomer shingling and paint than this vine, at present covering a whole side of some houses. I do not believe that the Ivy *never sear* is comparable to it. No wonder it has been extensively introduced into London. Let us have a good many Maples and Hickories and Scarlet Oaks, then, I say. Blaze away! Shall that dirty roll of bunting in the gun-house be all the colors a village can display? A village is not complete, unless it have these trees to mark the season in it. They are important, like the town-clock. A village that has them not will not be found to work well. It has a screw loose, an essential part is wanting. Let us have Willows for spring, Elms for summer, Maples and Walnuts and Tupeloes for autumn, Evergreens for winter, and Oaks for all seasons. What is a gallery in a house to a gallery in the streets, which every market-man rides through, whether he will or not? Of course, there is not a picture-gallery in the country which would be worth so much to us as is the western view at sunset under the Elms of our main street. They are the frame to a picture which almost daily is painted behind them. An avenue of elms as large as our largest and 3 miles long would seem to lead to some admirable place though only C———. were at the end of it.

A village needs these innocent stimulants of bright and cheering prospects to keep off melancholy and superstition. Show me two villages, one embowered in trees and blazing with all the glories of October, the other a merely trivial and treeless waste, or with only a single tree or 2 for suicides, and I shall be sure that in the latter will be found the most starved and bigoted religionists, and the most desperate drinkers. Every wash-tub, and milk-can, and grave-stone will be exposed. The inhabitants will disappear abruptly behind their barns and houses, like desert Arabs amid their rocks, and I shall look to see spears in their hands. They will be ready to accept the most barren and forlorn doctrine—as that the world is speedily coming to an end, or has already got to it, or that they themselves are turned wrong side outward. They will perchance crack their dry joints at one another and call it a spiritual communication.

But to confine ourselves to the Maples. What if we were to take half as much pains in protecting them as we do in setting them out! not stupidly tie our horses to our dahlia stems!

What meant the Fathers by establishing this *perfectly living* institution before the church? this institution which needs no repairing nor re-painting, which is continually "enlarged and repaired" by its growth?

Surely—they

> "*Wrought in a sad sincerity;*
> *Themselves from God they could not free;*
> *They* planted *better than they knew;*—
> *The conscious* trees *to beauty grew.*"

Verily these maples are cheap preachers, permanently settled, which preach their half-century, and century, aye and century and a half sermons, with constantly increasing unction and influence, ministering to many generations of men, and the least we can do is to supply them with suitable colleagues as they grow infirm.

THE SCARLET OAK

Belonging to a genus which is remarkable for the beautiful form of its leaves, I suspect that some Scarlet Oak leaves surpass those of all other Oaks in the rich and wild beauty of their outlines. I judge from an acquaintance with 12 species and from drawings which I have seen, of many others.

Stand under this tree and see how finely its leaves are cut against the sky, as it were, only a few sharp points extending from a midrib. They look like double, treble or quadruple

crosses. They are far more ethereal than the less deeply scolloped oak leaves. They have so little leafy terra-firma that they appear melting away in the light, and scarcely obstruct our view. The leaves of very young plants, are, like those of full grown oaks of other species, more entire, simple and lumpish in their outlines, but these, raised high on old trees, have solved the leafy problem. Lifted higher and higher and sublimated more and more, putting off some earthiness and cultivating more intimacy with the light each year, they have at length the least possible amount of earthy matter, and the greatest spread and grasp of skyey influences. There they dance, arm in arm with the light, tripping it on fantastic points, fit partners in those aerial halls. So intimately mingled are they with it, that what with their slenderness and their glossy surfaces, you can hardly tell at last what in the dance is leaf and what is light. And when no zephyr stirs, they are at most but a rich tracery to the forest windows.

I am again struck with their beauty, when, a month later they thickly strew the ground in the woods, piled one upon another under my feet. They are then brown above but purple beneath. With their narrow lobes and their bold deep scollops reaching almost to the middle, they suggest that the material must be cheap, or else there has been a lavish expense in their creation, as if so much had been cut out. Or else they seem to us, the remnants of the stuff out of which leaves have been cut

the ocean, whose extensive coast, alternate rounded bays with smooth strands, and sharp-pointed rocky capes, mark it as fitted for the habitation of man, and destined to become a centre of civilization at last. To the sailor's eye, it is a much-indented shore. Is it not, in fact, a shore to the aerial ocean, on which the windy surf beats? At sight of this leaf we are all mariners,—if not vikings, buccaneers, and filibusters. Both our love of repose and our spirit of adventure are addressed. In our most casual glance, perchance, we think, that, if we succeed in doubling those sharp capes, we shall find deep, smooth, and secure havens in the ample bays. How different from the White-Oak leaf, with its rounded headlands, on which no light-house need be placed! That is an England, with its long civil history, that may be read. This is some still unsettled New-found Island or Celebes. Shall we go and be rajahs there?

By the 26th of October the large Scarlet Oaks are in their prime, when other oaks are usually withered. They have been kindling their fires for a week past, and now generally burst into a blaze. This alone of *our* indigenous deciduous trees (excepting the Dogwood, of which I do not know half a dozen, and they are but large bushes), is now in its glory. The two Aspens and the Sugar Maple come nearest to it in date, but they have lost the greater part of their leaves. Of evergreens, only the pitch pine is still commonly bright.

But it requires a particular alertness, if not devotion to these phenomena, to appreciate the wide spread, but late and unexpected glory of the Scarlet Oaks. I do not speak here of the small trees and shrubs, which are commonly observed, and which are now withered, but of the large trees. Most go in and shut their doors, thinking that bleak and colorless November has already come, when some of the most brilliant and memorable colors are not yet lit.

This very perfect and vigorous one, about forty feet high, standing in an open pasture, which was quite glossy green on the 12th, is now, the 26th, completely changed to bright dark scarlet, every leaf, between you and the sun as if it had been dipped into a scarlet dye. The whole tree is much like a heart in form, as well as color. Was not this worth waiting for? Little did you think ten days ago, that that cold green tree would assume such color as this. Its leaves are still firmly attached, while those of other trees, are falling around it. It seems to say—I am the last to blush, but I blush deeper than any of ye. I bring up the rear in my red coat. We Scarlet ones, alone of oaks, have not given up the fight.

The sap is now, and even far into November, frequently flowing fast in these trees, as in Maples in the spring; and apparently their bright tints, now that most other Oaks are withered, are connected with this phenomenon. They are full of life. It has a pleasantly astringent, acorn-like taste, this strong Oak-wine, as I find on tapping them with my knife.

Looking across this woodland valley, a quarter of a mile wide, how rich those Scarlet Oaks, embosomed in Pines, their

bright red branches intimately intermingled with them! They
have their full effect there. The Pine-boughs are the green calyx
to their red petals. Or, as we go along a road in the woods, the
sun striking endwise through it, and lighting up the red tents
of the Oaks, which on each side are mingled with the liquid
green of the Pines, makes a very gorgeous scene. Indeed, without the evergreens for contrast, the autumnal tints would lose
much of their effect.

The Scarlet Oak asks a clear sky and the brightness of late
October days. These bring out its colors. If the sun goes into a
cloud, they become comparatively indistinct. As I sit on a cliff
in the southwest part of our town, the sun is now getting low,
and the woods in Lincoln, south and east of me, are lit up by
its more level rays; and in the Scarlet Oaks, scattered so equally
over the forest, there is brought out a more brilliant redness
than I had believed was in them. Every tree of this species
which is visible in those directions, even to the horizon, now
stands out distinctly red. Some great ones lift their red backs
high above the woods, in the next town, like huge roses with
a myriad of fine petals; and some more slender ones, in a small
grove of White Pines on Pine Hill in the east, on the very verge
of the horizon, alternating with the Pines on the edge of the
grove, and shouldering them with their red coats, look like
soldiers in red amid hunters in green. This time it is Lincoln
green, too. Till the sun got low, I did not believe that there
were so many redcoats in the forest army. Theirs is an intense

burning red, which would lose some of its strength, methinks, with every step you might take toward them; for the shade that lurks amid their foliage does not report itself at this distance,

and they are unanimously red. The focus of their reflected color is in the atmosphere far on this side. Every such tree becomes a nucleus of red, as it were, where, with the declining sun, that color grows and glows. It is partly borrowed fire, gathering strength from the sun on its way to your eye. It has only some comparatively dull red leaves for a rallying-point, or kindling-stuff, to start it, and it becomes an intense scarlet or red mist, or fire, which finds fuel for itself in the very atmosphere. So vivacious is redness. The very rails reflect a rosy light at this hour and season. You see a redder tree than exists.

If you wish to count the Scarlet Oaks, do it now. In a clear day stand thus on a hill-top in the woods, when the sun is an hour high, and every one within range of your vision, excepting in the west, will be revealed. You might live to the age of Methuselah and never find a tithe of them, otherwise. Yet sometimes even in a dark day I have thought them as bright as I ever saw them. Looking westward, their colors are lost in a blaze of light; but in other directions the whole forest is a flower-garden, in which these late roses burn, alternating with green, while the so-called "gardeners," walking here and there, perchance, beneath, with spade and water-pot, see only a few little asters amid withered leaves.

These are *my* China-asters, *my* late garden-flowers. It costs me nothing for a gardener. The falling leaves, all over the forest, are protecting the roots of my plants. Only look at what is to be seen, and you will have garden enough, without deepening the soil in your yard. We have only to elevate our view a little, to see the whole forest as a garden. The blossoming of the Scarlet Oak,—the forest-flower, surpassing all in splendor (at least since the Maple)! I do not know but they interest me more than the Maples, they are so widely and equally dispersed throughout the forest; they are so hardy, a nobler tree on the whole;—

our chief November flower, abiding the approach of winter with us, imparting warmth to early November prospects. It is remarkable that the latest bright color that is general should be this deep, dark scarlet and red, the intensest of colors. The ripest fruit of the year; like the cheek of a hard, glossy, red apple from the cold Isle of Orleans, which will not be mellow for eating till next spring! When I rise to a hill-top, a thousand of these great Oak roses, distributed on every side, as far as the horizon! I admire them four or five miles off! This my unfailing prospect for a fortnight past! This late forest-flower surpasses all that spring or summer could do. Their colors were but rare and dainty specks comparatively, (created for the near-sighted, who walk amid the humblest herbs and underwoods,) and made no impression on a distant eye. Now it is an extended forest or a mountain-side, through or along which we journey from day to day, that bursts into bloom. Comparatively, our gardening is on a petty scale,—the gardener still nursing a few asters amid dead weeds, ignorant of the gigantic asters and roses, which, as it were, overshadow him, and ask for none of his care. It is like a little red paint ground on a saucer, and held up against the sunset sky. Why not take more elevated and broader views, walk in the great garden, not skulk in a little "debauched" nook of it? consider the beauty of the forest, and not merely of a few impounded herbs?

Let your walks now be a little more adventurous; ascend the hills. If, about the last of October, you ascend any hill in the outskirts of our town, and probably of yours, and look over the forest, you may see——well, what I have endeavored to describe. All this you surely *will* see, and much more, if you are prepared to see it,—if you *look* for it. Otherwise, regular and universal as this phenomenon is, whether you stand on the hill-top or in the hollow, you will think for threescore years and ten that all the wood is, at this season, sear and brown. Objects are concealed from our view, not so much because they are out of the course of our visual ray as because we do not bring our minds and eyes to bear on them; for there is no power to see in the eye itself, any more than in any other jelly. We do not realize how far and widely, or how near and narrowly, we are to look. The greater part of the phenomena of Nature are for this reason concealed from us all our lives. The gardener sees only the gardener's garden. Here, too, as in political economy, the supply answers to the demand. Nature does not cast pearls before swine. There is just as much beauty visible to us in the landscape as we are prepared to appreciate,—not a grain more. The actual objects which one man will see from a particular hill-top are just as different from those which another will see as the beholders are different. The Scarlet Oak must, in a sense, be in your eye when you go forth. We cannot see any-thing until we are possessed with the idea of it, take it into our heads,—and then we can hardly see anything else. In my botanical rambles, I find that, first, the idea, or image, of a plant occupies my thoughts, though it may seem very foreign to this

locality—no nearer than Hudson's Bay—and for some weeks or months I go thinking of it, and expecting it, unconsciously, and at length I surely see it. This, is the history of my finding a score or more of rare plants, which I could name.

A man sees only what concerns him. A botanist absorbed in the study of grasses, does not distinguish the grandest pasture oaks. He, as it were, tramples down oaks unwittingly in his walk, or at most sees only their shadows. I have found that it required a different intention of the eye, in the same locality, to see different plants, even when they were closely allied,—as *Juncaceae* and *Gramineae*;—when I was looking for the former, I did not see the latter, in their midst. How much more then it requires different intentions of the eye and of the mind, to attend to different departments of knowledge! How differently the poet and the naturalist look at objects!

Take a New England Select Man, and set him on the highest of our hills, and tell him to look—sharpening his sight to the utmost, and putting on the glasses that suit him best, (aye, using a spy-glass, if he likes),—and make a full report. What, probably, will he *spy*?—what will he *select* to look at? Of course, he will see a Brocken spectre of himself. He will see several meeting-houses, at least, and perhaps that somebody ought to be assessed higher than he is, since he has so handsome a woodlot. Now take Julius Caesar—or Emanuel Swedenborg—or a Fejee Islander, and set him up there! Or suppose all together and let them compare notes afterward. Will it appear that they have enjoyed the same prospect? What they will see will be as different as Rome was from Heaven or Hell, or the last from the Fejee Islands.— For aught we know, as strange a man as any of these, is always at our elbow.

Why, it takes a sharp shooter to bring down even such trivial game, as snipes and woodcocks, he must take very particular aim, and know what he is aiming at. He would stand a very small chance, if he fired at random into the sky, being told that snipes were flying there. And so is it with him that shoots at beauty; though he wait till the sky falls, he will not bag any, if he does not already know its seasons and haunts, and the color of its wing,—if he has not dreamed of it, so that he can *anticipate* it; then, indeed, he flushes it at every step, shoots double and on the wing, with both barrels, even in cornfields. The sportsman trains himself, dresses and watches unweariedly, and loads and primes for his particular game. He prays for it, and offers sacrifices, and so he gets it. After due and long preparation, schooling his eye and hand, dreaming awake and asleep, with gun and paddle and boat he goes out after meadow-hens, which most of his townsmen never saw nor dreamed of, and paddles for miles against a head-wind, and wades in water up to his knees, being out all day without his dinner, and *therefore* he gets them. He had them half-way into his bag when he started, and has only to shove them down. The true sportsman can shoot you almost any of his game from his windows: what else has he windows or eyes for? It comes and perches at last on the barrel of his gun; but the rest of the world never see it *with the feathers on.* The geese fly exactly under his zenith, and honk when they get there, and he will keep himself supplied by firing up his chimney; twenty musquash have the refusal of each one of his traps before it is empty. If he lives, and his game-spirit increases, heaven and earth shall fail him sooner than game; and when he dies, he will go to more extensive, and, perchance, happier hunting-grounds. The fisherman, too, dreams of fish, sees a bobbing cork in his dreams, till he can almost catch them in his sink spout. I knew a girl who, being sent to pick huckleberries, picked wild gooseberries by the quart, where no one else knew that there were any, because she was accustomed to pick them up country where she came from. The astronomer knows where to go star-gathering, and sees one clearly in his mind before any have seen it with a glass. The hen scratches and finds her food right under where she stands, but such is not the way with the hawk.

———

These bright leaves which I have mentioned are not the exception but the rule, for I believe that all leaves, even grasses and mosses, acquire brighter colors just before their fall. When you come to observe faithfully the changes of each humblest plant, you find that each has sooner or later its peculiar autumnal tint, and if you undertake to make a complete list of the bright tints it will be nearly as long as a catalogue of the plants in your vicinity.

Acknowledgments

I have wanted to do this book—to put a spotlight on Thoreau's most enthusiastic piece of writing—for a long time. *Walden* is enthusiastic in places, but "Autumnal Tints" is ecstatic all through. So when Lincoln Perry recently agreed to do a suite of paintings for the book, the project took off. I am grateful to my agent and friend, Tim Seldes, for his unending faith in the project, and I'm grateful to another painter, Henryk Fantazos, for introducing me to the work of Anita Albus. I thank my editor at Norton, Alane Mason, for her steady support and for her fine, old-fashioned, detailed, substantive editing. Her work and that of her multitalented, cheerful, and hardworking assistant, Denise Scarfi, made the details of producing this book a series of pleasures. Thanks also to Mark Melnick for making this a a beautiful volume.

R.D.R

Personal Leaves

We have left room for a few leaves of your own choosing. To keep the color from fading, you will need an iron and some wax paper. Put the leaf between two pieces of wax paper. Set the iron on Warm. Using a thin cloth or a thick paper layer on top of the leaf sandwich, iron each side for ten seconds or so. You can cut around the pressed leaf with scissors, leaving a wax edge as a seal, or you can peel off the wax paper, which will leave a coat of wax on the leaf.